Life's better at the beach

sandy gingras

Published by Sourcebooks, Inc.
P.O. Box 4410, Naperville, Illinois 60567–4410
(630) 961–3900
Fax: (630) 961–2168
www.sourcebooks.com

Printed and bound in China.
LEO 10 9 8 7 6 5 4 3 2 1

"The beach is where my heart is."

Life's better at the beach.

and life is simple and sweet.

and let go.

We remember to just be.

And it's clear that Life's better at the beach not only because the beach is an escape from reality, but because the beach is a reminder of what Life should be more about.

In our hearts,
we long
for this
beachy
kind of
existence
all year
long--

where all we need
in life is in our
beach bag, and a
whole world
exists under
our beach
umbrella.

The beach is a
state of mind,
a place as emotional
as it is geographic.

Let's dive into our dreams.

Let's say,
"No worries."

Let's lean toward sunshine,

give our ideas wings,

and let ourselves go
a little out to sea.

Let's say, "Anchors away" to everything that's holding us back.

Let's hold onto each other,

Let's let the
Sea

into our hearts,

Let's wake up to the dawn, Linger over the day, Swoon over the sunset. Let's undo the schedule.

Let's be as passionate

as a summer storm.

Let's glide.

Let's lose the uncomfortable shoes.

Let's wear a
big sun hat and
Jackie O sunglasses
and tell everyone,
"Don't bother me, I'm napping."

Let's rest and recline, rejuvenate and recharge. Let's twiddle our thumbs.

Let's beguile the time. Let's Lounge.
Let's while away the hours...

Let's connect back to our hearts.

REALITY

BEACH

Let's not allow realism to get in the way of our dreams.

Let's get it
(at last)
that
imperfection
is
beauty.

Let's seek horizons

and wish on stars.

Let's remember that happiness is a journey, not a destination.

Let's

find a silver lining
in every cloud,

because there's better weather ahead.

Let's let the hard stuff
soften and fade.

Let's stop to let the duck family cross the road.

Let's recess!

Let's dive under the

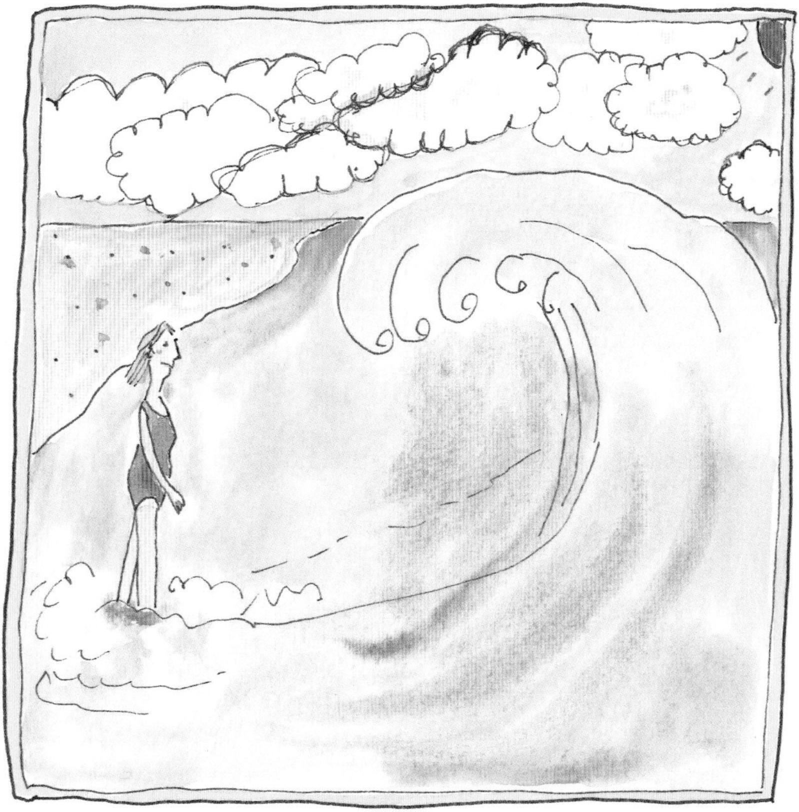

big waves,

and come out on the
other side

Laughing.

Let's give ourselves a
little place to just
dream.

Since she was a little girl, Sandy Gingras has been doodling and writing stories, trying to figure out life's mysteries (her hero is still Nancy Drew). She lives in a happy cottage on the bay on an island in New Jersey with her almost-grown-up son and a wonderful golden retriever and two ridiculous cats. You can read more about Sandy and what she does at www.how-to-live.com.